EVIL And the OCCULT

A 4-week course to help Christian teenagers protect themselves against the trap of Satanism

by Rick Lawrence

Group®

Loveland, Colorado

Evil and the Occult
Copyright © 1990 by Group Publishing, Inc.

Second Printing, 1990

Credits
Edited by Stephen Parolini
Cover designed by Jill Bendykowski and DeWain Stoll
Interior designed by Jan Aufdemberge and Judy Atwood Bienick
Illustrations by Ron Wheeler
Cover photo by David Priest and Brenda Rundback

ISBN 1-55945-102-5
Printed in the United States of America

CONTENTS

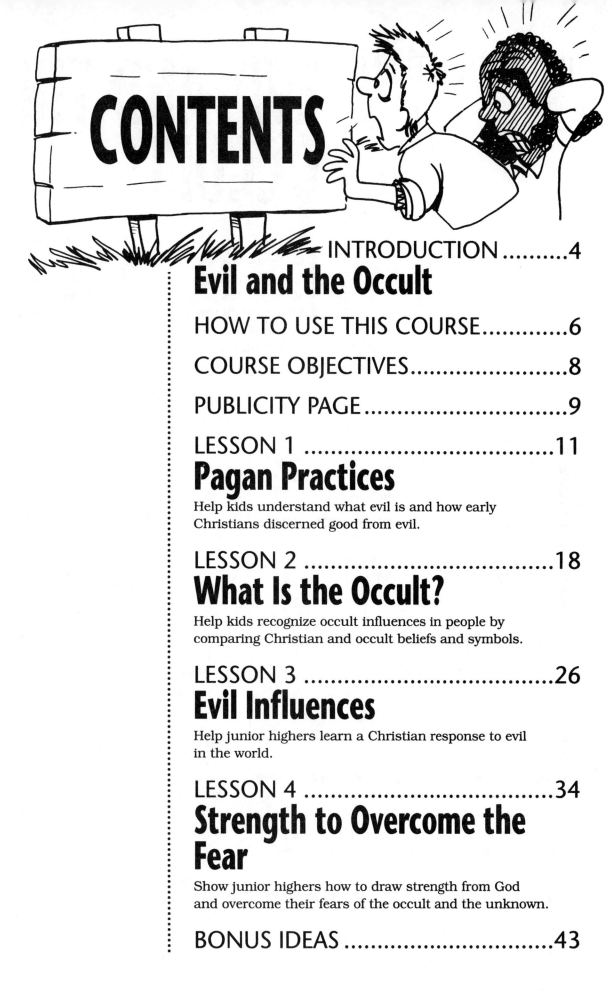

EVIL AND THE OCCULT

Jim heard the voice inside his head, the one that always told him to prove himself. "Do it now!" Jim felt the bat strike Steve's face. As they chased him down, Steve stumbled through the dark, asking his pursuers the same thing over and over. "Why me, you guys? Why me?" It took them a few minutes to catch up to him. Ron was laughing. "Because it's fun, Steve," he said.

When the frenzy was over, Steve was still moaning. Jim took his bloody bat and nudged him in the shoulder. "Sacrifice to Satan," he said.

• • •

Three small-town kids in Missouri confessed to beating a friend to death with baseball bats. The group's leader, Jim Hardy, told police a "voice" commanded him to kill.

It didn't take much of a nudge for Jim to fall under the influence of the occult. Next to the promises of the occult, it seemed God and the church had little to offer.

Sadly, Jim Hardy's story is just one of many.

The occult is one of the most visible manifestations of evil in the world. To junior highers who're searching to fill a void in their lives, the occult can seem appealing. Yet dabbling in the occult can be dangerous.

Junior highers are exposed to evil in other ways too. Some get involved with fantasy role-playing games or listen to heavy metal music that's laced with Satanic imagery. Others are intrigued by horror movies and even look at the evil killers in the films as "heroes."

Many junior highers are fascinated with evil. And knowing the difference between evil and good isn't always easy.

Kids need to know how to stand up to evil and the occult. It's the church's responsibility to help.

Vermont—A 15-year-old girl dies after firing a bullet into her brain. She reportedly leaves a note confessing her devotion to Satan.

Georgia—A 15-year-old girl is strangled by three teenagers, allegedly as a sacrifice to Satan.

New Jersey—A 14-year-old boy fatally stabs his mother then kills himself. Police point to his fascination with Satan as the primary influence to kill.

New York—A 17-year-old boy is murdered by two teenagers. Later it's discovered that the two teenagers were involved in a Satanic cult.

This 4-week course will help your junior highers and middle schoolers understand evil in the world. They'll see the deception and false promises the occult offers. They'll learn how to discern good from evil. And they'll discover they can turn to God when they're in need.

HOW TO USE THIS COURSE

ACTIVE
LEARNING

Think back on an important lesson you've learned. Did you learn it from reading about it? from hearing about it? from something you experienced? Chances are, the most important lessons you've learned came from something you experienced. That's what active learning is—learning by doing. And active learning is a key element in Group's Active Bible Curriculum.

Active learning leads students in doing things that help them understand important principles, messages and ideas. It's a discovery process that helps kids internalize what they learn.

Each lesson section in Group's Active Bible Curriculum plays an important part in active learning.

The **Opener** involves kids in the topic in fun and unusual ways.

The **Action and Reflection** includes an experience designed to evoke specific feelings in the students. This section also processes those feelings through "How did you feel?" questions and applies the message to situations kids face.

The **Bible Application** actively connects the topic with the Bible. It helps kids see how the Bible is relevant to the situations they face.

The **Commitment** helps students internalize the Bible's message and commit to make changes in their lives.

The **Closing** funnels the lesson's message into a time of creative reflection and prayer.

When you put all the sections together, you get a lesson that's fun to teach—and kids get messages they'll remember.

**BEFORE THE
4-WEEK
SESSION**

● Read the Introduction, the Course Objectives and This Course at a Glance (p. 8).

● Decide how you'll publicize the course using the art on the Publicity Page (p. 9). Prepare fliers, newsletter articles and posters as needed.

● Look at the Bonus Ideas (p. 43) and decide which ones you'll use.

• Read the opening statements, Objectives and Bible Basis for the lesson. The Bible Basis shows how specific passages relate to junior highers today.

• Choose which Opener and Closing options to use. Each is appropriate for a different kind of group. The first option is often more active.

• Gather necessary supplies from This Lesson at a Glance.

• Read each section of the lesson. Adjust where necessary for your class size and meeting room.

BEFORE EACH LESSON

• The approximate minutes listed give you an idea of how long each activity will take. Each lesson is designed to take 35 to 60 minutes. Shorten or lengthen activities as needed to fit your group.

• If you see you're going to have extra time, do an activity or two from the "If You Still Have Time" box or from the Bonus Ideas (p. 43).

• Dive into the activities with the students. Don't be a spectator. The lesson will be more successful and rewarding to both you and your students.

HELPFUL HINTS

• The answers given after discussion questions are responses your students *might* give. They aren't the only answers or the "right" answers. If needed, use them to spark discussion. Kids won't always say what you wish they'd say. That's why some of the responses given are negative or controversial. If someone responds negatively, don't be shocked. Accept the person, and use the opportunity to explore other angles of the issue.

COURSE OBJECTIVES

By the end of this course your students will:
- understand how early Christians dealt with evil;
- learn how to discern good from evil;
- learn about the occult and how to avoid it;
- discover the differences between Christianity and the occult;
- understand Satan's influence on society and how to fight it;
- learn how to draw strength from God; and
- find the peace of God's protection.

THIS COURSE AT A GLANCE

Before you dive into the lessons, familiarize yourself with each lesson aim. Then read the scripture passages.
- Study them as a background to the lessons.
- Use them as a basis for your personal devotions.
- Think about how they relate to kids' circumstances today.

LESSON 1: PAGAN PRACTICES
Lesson Aim: To help kids understand what evil is and how early Christians discerned good from evil.
Bible Basis: Acts 8:9-24; 17:16-29; and Revelation 12:7-9.

LESSON 2: WHAT IS THE OCCULT?
Lesson Aim: To help kids recognize occult influences in people by comparing Christian and occult beliefs and symbols.
Bible Basis: Matthew 8:28-34 and 2 Corinthians 11:13-15.

LESSON 3: EVIL INFLUENCES
Lesson Aim: To help junior highers learn a Christian response to evil in the world.
Bible Basis: John 8:42-47; Colossians 2:8-14; and 1 John 2:15-18, 21-24.

LESSON 4: STRENGTH TO OVERCOME THE FEAR
Lesson Aim: To show junior highers how to draw strength from God and overcome their fears of evil and the unknown.
Bible Basis: Psalm 23; John 16:33; and Romans 8:31-39.

PUBLICITY PAGE

Grab your junior highers' attention! Copy this page, then cut and paste the art of your choice in your church bulletin or newsletter to advertise this course on evil and the occult. Or copy and use the ready-made flier as a bulletin insert.

Splash this art on posters, fliers or even postcards! Just add the vital details: the date and time the course begins, and where you'll meet.

It's that simple.

A 4-week junior high course on how to respond to evil in the world

Come to _____

On _____

At _____

Discover how God's strength can help you overcome your fears.

PAGAN PRACTICES

Friends plead: "Just try one of these pills; you'll forget all the problems you're having in math."

Television preaches: "The more money you have, the happier you are."

Parents fume: "If you don't start working on your grades now, you'll never make it into a good college; you'll be a nobody!"

Good and evil aren't always black and white. Evil is often disguised as good, and it's sometimes hard for junior highers and middle schoolers to stand for the truth.

LESSON AIM

To help kids understand what evil is and how early Christians discerned good from evil.

OBJECTIVES

Students will:
- **learn that Satan's main weapon is deception;**
- **see how God's truths are stronger than Satan's lies;**
- **discover modern-day idols we worship; and**
- **learn to trust in God's Word.**

BIBLE BASIS

ACTS 8:9-24
ACTS 17:16-29
REVELATION 12:7-9

Look up the following scriptures. Then read the background paragraphs to see how the passages relate to your junior highers or middle schoolers.

In **Acts 8:9-24**, a magician tries to buy healing powers.

In Peter's time, many magicians, prophets and healers claimed to have supernatural power. The people were hungry for power. That's why many of them initially followed Jesus.

But just like today, many people sought power for wrong reasons. They wanted power alone and didn't pay much attention to where it came from.

Kids want all the power they can get to face their confusing, sometimes frightening world. But they need to look at the hand that's offering them power before they accept.

In **Acts 17:16-29**, Paul shows the intellectuals that they worship false gods, while he worships the one, true God.

Many of the idols of Paul's day represented a mixture of Greek and Roman mythology. The man-made idols presented a world run by many different gods.

Junior highers and middle schoolers live in a world of many false gods. Sports stars, musicians, drugs, fame, even the "cool" kids at school—all have kids bowing down before them. Kids need to learn to see beyond the attractive, tempting exteriors of the false gods.

In **Revelation 12:7-9**, Satan loses a war in heaven.

God—not Satan—won the battle in heaven. But sometimes God's truths seem less dramatic, less important or less desirable than the temptations Satan offers.

That's why many kids choose to serve and worship false gods rather than the one, true God. They need to understand the different kind of power and strength God gives.

THIS LESSON AT A GLANCE

Section	Minutes	What Students Will Do	Supplies
Opener (Option 1)	5 to 10	**Pick the Fake**—Pick out the fake fruit using only one sense.	Real and fake fruit, gloves, blindfold, cotton, clothespins
(Option 2)		**Paper Clip Challenge**—Bend a paper clip and try to fool other students.	Paper clips, marker
Action and Reflection	10 to 15	**Power Play**—Choose which item represents the most power.	Magazines, newspapers, scissors, steel trash can, paper, pencils, matches
Bible Application	10 to 15	**Exposing Frauds**—Read and discuss how Christians discerned truth from lies.	Bibles, chalkboard or newsprint, chalk or marker, paper, pencils
Commitment	5 to 10	**Idol Search**—Pick out the idols hidden in a picture of a normal family.	"Idol Search" handouts (p. 17), pencils
Closing (Option 1)	5 to 10	**Paper-Clipped Truth**—Use paper clips to spell out one word that represents God's truth.	Paper clips
(Option 2)		**Trash Your Idols**—Throw a paper airplane with a list of idols into the trash.	"Idol Search" handouts from Idol Search, trash can

The Lesson

OPTION 1: PICK THE FAKE

Line up several pieces of real fruit—and one piece of fake fruit—on a table. Ask for five volunteers. Have them each pick a different sense—sight, hearing, touch, smell—all except taste. Block off all but the one sense each person has chosen. Then have each person try to pick the fake fruit using only the sense he or she has chosen.

For example, here's how to block off the other senses of the person who chooses sight. Put cotton in the ears, gloves on the hands, a clothespin on the nose and instruct him or her not to taste the fruit. In the same way, block off the appropriate senses of the other participants.

After all the volunteers have made their choices one at a time, show everyone the one piece of fake fruit.

Ask:

● **Which sense gives you the best clue to the fake fruit? Explain.** (Touch, you can feel the difference between wax and real fruit; smell, fake fruit doesn't smell like fruit.)

● **Is it hard to pick out the fake if you're not allowed to get too close to the fruit? Why or why not?** (Yes, the outside can look just like real fruit; no, I can tell a fake a mile away.)

Read aloud Psalm 34:8.

Say: **The best way to tell whether God is the "real" God is to "taste" him. That means to explore him up close. Sometimes the world we live in wants us to worship false gods—gods Satan has placed in our midst. And it's hard to know they're false because we can't "taste" everything in life. So things may look good on the outside—like drugs—but be fake and rotten inside.**

OPTION 2: PAPER CLIP CHALLENGE

Before the session, take a paper clip and bend it into an unusual form. Then subtly mark one end with a black marker. Form a circle and give each person a paper clip. Show your bent paper clip to kids at close range, but hide the mark you made on it.

Say: **I'm going to give my paper clip to the person next to me. That person should quickly bend his or her paper clip to look just like mine, without letting anyone else see which is the original and which is the copy. Then that person should turn to the next person in the circle and ask him or her to choose the original. After that person chooses between the two, he or she should bend his or her paper clip to look just like the one chosen, then ask** the next person to choose the original. We'll continue around the circle until it's my turn again.

When it's your turn, find your original paper clip. More than likely, someone at some point picked a copy. Show kids the mark you made on the paper clip.

Ask:

● **How hard was it to tell the difference between the original and the copy?**

● **What's the only sure way you could find which paper clip was the original?** (There's no way to tell; ask the person who made the original.)

Say: **Sometimes it's hard to know what's real and what's an imitation. God is real, but Satan has made many cheap, hollow imitations. The only way to tell the original from the fake is to ask the Creator—God.**

ACTION AND REFLECTION
(10 to 15 minutes)

POWER PLAY

Hand out magazines, newspapers and scissors to students. Ask kids to cut out pictures or headlines that represent power to them, such as money, health clubs, weapons, politicians, business people, universities. As kids look for pictures and headlines, place a match on a table in front of them.

After five minutes or so, gather the clippings and place them on the table in front of kids. Form three groups and pass out a piece of paper and a pencil to each group.

Say: **Each group should rank the items on this table from most powerful to least powerful. On your paper, write the most powerful item at the top and work your way down the paper to the least powerful item.**

Allow kids to look at the items, and encourage group discussion. After about five minutes, ask each group to tell about its ranking. Compare the three lists and ask the entire group to vote on a most powerful and least powerful item. If the group chooses the match as the most powerful, congratulate them.

Otherwise, say: **Your lists are all well-thought-out. But the most powerful item on the table was this match.**

Pick up the match.

Say: **Let me demonstrate.**

Take kids outside. Dump all the clippings into a steel trash can. Light the match and set fire to the clippings. Or light just a corner of one clipping to illustrate the point.

Ask:

● **How did you feel when I showed you the power of the match? Why?** (Surprised, I didn't expect it; confused, I didn't know what it meant.)

● **How is this match like God's power?** (It's real; it can overcome other powers.)

Say: **The clippings were just pictures of the real thing. They had no real power. But the match was the real thing. It had power. Satan tries to fool us the same way. He** shows us pictures of things we think are powerful—like the magical powers in horror movies or on television—and convinces us these things are better and more powerful than what God has to offer. But Satan is a liar. And God is holding a match.

EXPOSING FRAUDS

Say: **It's sometimes easy to be deceived into believing something is true when it's really false. And we aren't the only ones who've been taken in by deception. Early Christians had the same trouble. Even though they'd seen Jesus in person and had witnessed his power and heard the truth of his words, they were still tempted to believe in Satan's false gods.**

Form groups of no larger than four. Assign each group one of the following scripture passages:
- Acts 8:9-24
- Revelation 12:7-9
- Acts 17:16-29

Have groups each read their passage. While they're reading, write the following discussion questions on a chalkboard or newsprint:

For Acts 8:9-24:
- Why was Simon fascinated with the healings he saw?
- What was Simon's motive in asking the disciples for their power?
- Why did Peter criticize Simon?

For Acts 17:16-29:
- Do you think it's easier to worship a material object—like an idol—than to worship a God you can't see with your eyes? Why or why not?
- Why was Paul so confident God was real and living?

For Revelation 12:7-9:
- Why do you think Satan tried to take over heaven?
- Why did God's angels throw Satan to Earth?
- What do you think Satan's attitude toward God's children—you and me—is?

Have students write their answers to the questions on paper, then talk about them within their groups. Have groups report their discoveries.

IDOL SEARCH

Say: **In 1 Corinthians 12:1-3, Paul says the people followed "mute idols" before they followed Jesus. Idols were statues—made of stone or wood—that people put their faith and trust in. People looked to these dead objects for comfort, guidance and power.**

Give each person an "Idol Search" handout (p. 17). Have kids complete the handout.

Gather together and ask students to explain why they circled certain objects on the handout. Then have students each

BIBLE APPLICATION
(10 to 15 minutes)

COMMITMENT
(5 to 10 minutes)

choose one thing they circled that they've been tempted to make into an idol. Have them turn over their handouts and write a commitment to God to turn away from that idol.

Form a circle. Have kids each, one by one, place their paper in the center of the circle. As they return to the circle, have them face outward. Then say: **When we turn away from idols, we need to turn toward God and he will shower us with his love.**

Go around the circle, saying one thing you're thankful for related to each student. As you thank kids, turn them back around to face inward. Have kids put their arms around each other for a group hug.

CLOSING
(5 to 10 minutes)

OPTION 1: PAPER-CLIPPED TRUTH

Form groups of three. Give each group a supply of paper clips. Ask groups each to arrange the paper clips on the table to spell out a word (or words) that represents God's truth or goodness, such as Jesus, Holy Spirit, love, Bible.

Then have each group explain its word. Ask someone from each group to close in prayer by thanking God for the word his or her group formed.

OPTION 2: TRASH YOUR IDOLS

Have students make paper airplanes out of their "Idol Search" handouts. Line students against a wall, and place a trash can 10 to 20 feet away from them. Have kids each, one by one, fly their airplane into the trash can. Allow them to get as close as they need to so they can fly it into the trash can. Then have them each repeat after you:

God, I'll throw these idols away, so I can follow you alone.

If You Still Have Time . . .

Taste Test Challenge—Do a cola taste test using Coke, Pepsi, RC, and a generic or local cola. Have kids taste each cola and see if they can pick out which is the Coke.

Then ask:

● **Could you pick Coke out of a lineup if you tasted it each time before you tasted each of the others? Why or why not?**

● **What does this tell us about how we should get to know God—the real thing?**

Idol Mobile—Have kids pick pictures from magazines or newspapers of things people make into idols. Then draw a "No Idols" sign on paper and use string to create a "No Idols" mobile.

IDOL SEARCH

Circle the objects in the picture that could be worshiped as idols.

LESSON 2

WHAT IS THE OCCULT?

Satan uses a powerful tool to draw young people into the occult—deception. He makes himself—and the things he does—look attractive to kids who are searching for meaning and control in an out-of-control world.

The best way to strip the occult of its power is to understand how Satan tries to deceive.

LESSON AIM

To help kids recognize occult influences in people by comparing Christian and occult beliefs and symbols.

OBJECTIVES

Students will:
- learn how Satan disguises evil by making it look good on the outside;
- do a simple pantomime on how Satan tempted Jesus;
- learn how Christians and satanists differ; and
- learn about the meanings behind occultic and Christian symbols.

BIBLE BASIS

MATTHEW 8:28-34
LUKE 4:1-13
2 CORINTHIANS 11:10-15

Look up the following scriptures. Then read the background paragraphs to see how the passages relate to your junior highers or middle schoolers.

In **Matthew 8:28-34**, Jesus confronts two demon-possessed men and casts the demons into pigs.

The demon-possessed men were so fearsome and violent that people were afraid to pass by their territory. But Jesus wasn't afraid of them because he knew God had authority over Satan's servants. The demons quaked before Jesus.

Sometimes kids are bullied into thinking the occult is more powerful than God's truth. But it's not.

In **Luke 4:1-13**, Satan tempts Jesus in the wilderness.

Satan, in his arrogance, believed he could deceive Jesus with the same things he'd been deceiving humans with for thousands of years—pride, power and rebellion. Jesus refused to argue with Satan. He simply quoted the truth from scripture and walked on.

Sometimes kids are vulnerable to the lies of the occult because they're not confident of the truth. They need to learn that the truth comes from knowing who God is and what he desires.

In **2 Corinthians 11:10-15**, Satan disguises himself as an angel.

Satan draws people into the occult by disguising evil as something good. The New Age Movement, for example, is influenced by occultic practices.

Junior highers are prone to make emotional, snap decisions. They don't often think of the long-term consequences of their actions—so the occult is a temptation to them. They must learn to strip away the disguises of evil.

THIS LESSON AT A GLANCE

Section	Minutes	What Students Will Do	Supplies
Opener (Option 1)	5 to 10	**Truth in Advertising?**—Design deceptive ads for dangerous things.	Magazines, scissors, glue, posterboard, markers
(Option 2)		**Evil in Disguise**—Create and wear quick disguises.	Old clothes, hats, shoes, sheets, M&M candies
Action and Reflection	10 to 15	**Evil and Good at War**—Pantomime Jesus' temptation in the wilderness.	"The Big Lie" script (p. 24)
Bible Application	10 to 15	**Enemy/Friend Descriptions**—Write descriptions of Satan, God and those who follow them.	Paper, pencils, Bibles, marker, newsprint
Commitment	5 to 10	**Grappling Graphics**—Compare Christian and occult symbols.	"Light and Dark" handouts (p. 25), pencils, tape, trash can
Closing (Option 1)	5 to 10	**Communion Prayer**—Participate in a communion ceremony.	Communion elements
(Option 2)		**God's Power Ads**—Design ads that illustrate God's power.	Magazines, scissors, glue, markers, construction paper

The Lesson

OPTION 1: TRUTH IN ADVERTISING?

Give students magazines, scissors, glue, posterboard and markers. Have them each design an ad—for something bad or dangerous—that makes the "product" look good. Products could include: drugs, poison, hand grenades, nuclear war or swimming in a pool of alligators. For example, someone could design an ad for drugs that says "Leave Your Troubles Behind You" and pictures a happy person.

Have kids each display and talk about their ad.

Ask:

● **How are these ads like real ads you see on television or in newspapers and magazines?** (Both play up the positive.)

● **How are they different?** (These are more obviously lies; real ads are more subtle.)

Say: **Sometimes advertisers don't tell you the whole story because they're afraid you won't buy their product if you know the consequences of using it. In the same way, we're often drawn into evil by outwardly attractive benefits that hide terrible consequences.**

OPTION 2: EVIL IN DISGUISE

Form a circle and pile a supply of old clothes, hats, shoes and sheets in the center.

Say: **Imagine you're a criminal on the run from the law. You have three minutes and these materials to make a disguise. When the police arrive, you'll need to slip past them unnoticed or risk arrest. Go!**

After three minutes, have students each model their disguise. Then have kids vote for the most creative one; don't let kids vote for themselves. Award the winner a package of M&M candies—the shell disguises the chocolate within!

Ask:

● **What are some of evil's disguises?** (Lust; greed; selfishness; pride.)

● **How do you feel when you realize you've been tricked?** (Angry; upset; stupid.)

● **How are people tricked into following evil?** (They're fooled into thinking something's good for them when it's not; they're promised great things.)

Say: **Evil in the world is often disguised to look appealing. The only way to know if something is evil is to tear away the disguise. During this lesson we'll attempt to tear away the disguises worn by the occult.**

EVIL AND GOOD AT WAR

Ask for two volunteers to read a short skit. Give them copies of "The Big Lie" script (p. 24). Then form two groups: one to play Jesus and one to play Satan. Have the groups line up facing each other. As the skit is read, have the groups silently act out their parts. Have one volunteer read Satan's part. Have the other volunteer read Jesus' part. Tell the readers to read slowly, pausing to allow the actors to act out the story. Encourage kids to put themselves into their parts. Either you or another student may read the narrator's part.

Ask:

● **Why were Satan's offers tempting?** (They were things Jesus might've wanted.)

● **How did Jesus know he shouldn't do what Satan asked him to do?** (He knew Satan was a liar; he knew God's Word; he trusted God.)

● **Some people say everyone will sell out for a certain price. What temptations might entice you to follow Satan?** (Money; fame; power; love; feeling like I belong.)

Say: **Many people are enticed into occult practices because they want power—or they want to feel like they belong. But they don't really know what they're getting into. Next we'll look at how Jesus and Satan compare as leaders.**

ENEMY/FRIEND DESCRIPTIONS

Form three groups and give each group a piece of paper and a pencil. Have groups each read the following scriptures:

● Matthew 8:28-34   ● 2 Corinthians 11:10-15
● Luke 4:1-13

Then ask groups each to write—based upon what they already know—five things that describe Satan or those who follow him, such as evil, liar or deceiver. After that, have them each write five things that describe God or those who follow him, such as loving, kind or healer.

Label one sheet of newsprint "A Picture of God" and another sheet of newsprint "A Picture of Satan." Gather back together and combine the appropriate descriptions on the two sheets of newsprint.

Ask:

● **How do these "pictures" compare?** (They're drastically different, Jesus looks good and Satan looks terrible.)

● **If you'd never heard of Jesus or Satan, who would you choose to follow based on these descriptions? Why?** (Jesus, because he helps people; Satan, because it seems he has fun.)

● **Which picture describes someone who'd make a good friend? Explain.** (God's, because he cares for people; God's, because he's honest and kind; Satan's, because he can offer lots of fun times.)

● **Which is better—following someone you'd trust as a**

friend or following someone you couldn't trust? Explain.
(Following someone you trust, because you can feel confident
in where you're going; someone you trust, because you won't
feel scared of what might happen to you.)

Say: **Choosing to get involved in the occult is choosing
Satan as your leader. But choosing to become a Christian
is choosing to follow Jesus.**

COMMITMENT
(5 to 10 minutes)

GRAPPLING GRAPHICS

Give students each a "Light and Dark" handout (p. 25).

Say: **The occult symbols on the right side of your handout each have an explanation. The Christian symbols on
the left side of the handout don't have explanations. Look
at what each occult symbol signifies, then try to match it
with a Christian symbol that signifies the exact opposite.
Draw a line between the two. Then, next to each Christian symbol, write what you think that symbol represents.**

Ask:

● **What are some differences between the occult symbols and the Christian symbols?** (Occult symbols signify
dark, evil, gruesome things; Christian symbols signify love,
community, trust, goodness.)

● **How does the occult draw on Christian, biblical imagery in its symbols and practices?** (It twists what's good
about Christianity into something bad.)

Have kids each tear out one Christian symbol and tape it to
a notebook, book or other personal item as a sign of their allegiance to God and his ways. Have kids form a circle around
a trash can. Have them each, one at a time, throw away the
rest of their handout. As each person throws away the handout, say: **You don't need the occult to feel worthwhile. For
God loves you and has given you special qualities.**

Have kids each tell two or three positive qualities about
each other.

CLOSING
(5 to 10 minutes)

OPTION 1: COMMUNION PRAYER

Form a circle around a table and have a communion service as a sign of allegiance to God. Be sure to follow your
church's policies concerning the service. Close by praying the
Lord's Prayer together.

OPTION 2: GOD'S POWER ADS

Give students magazines, scissors, glue, markers and construction paper. Ask them each to design an ad that illus-
trates God's power. Have kids display and talk about their
ads, then close in prayer by thanking God for one way he's
overcome evil with his great power.

If You Still Have Time . . .

Hide the Light—Form two teams. Give Team #1 a flashlight, and ask Team #2 to leave the room for a few minutes. Have Team #1 turn on the flashlight; then give team members two minutes to hide it somewhere the other team won't be able to find it when the lights are turned off. When time is up, bring Team #2 back in, turn off the lights and tell members of Team #2 they have two minutes to find the flashlight. Team #1 wins if Team #2 doesn't find the flashlight in two minutes. Team #2 wins if it finds the flashlight within two minutes.

Tell kids that darkness can't hide a strong light for long, just as evil can't stand up to God for long.

Twisted Evil—Form teams of no more than three. Have teams each copy the following scrambled words onto a piece of paper.

- vole
- uhtrt
- mdferoe
- fcromto
- yemcr

Say: **Satan's way is to take what's good and twist it into something bad. On "go," begin unscrambling the words. Each word describes a quality of God. The first team to unscramble all five words wins.**

The answers are: love, truth, freedom, comfort and mercy.

THE BIG LIE

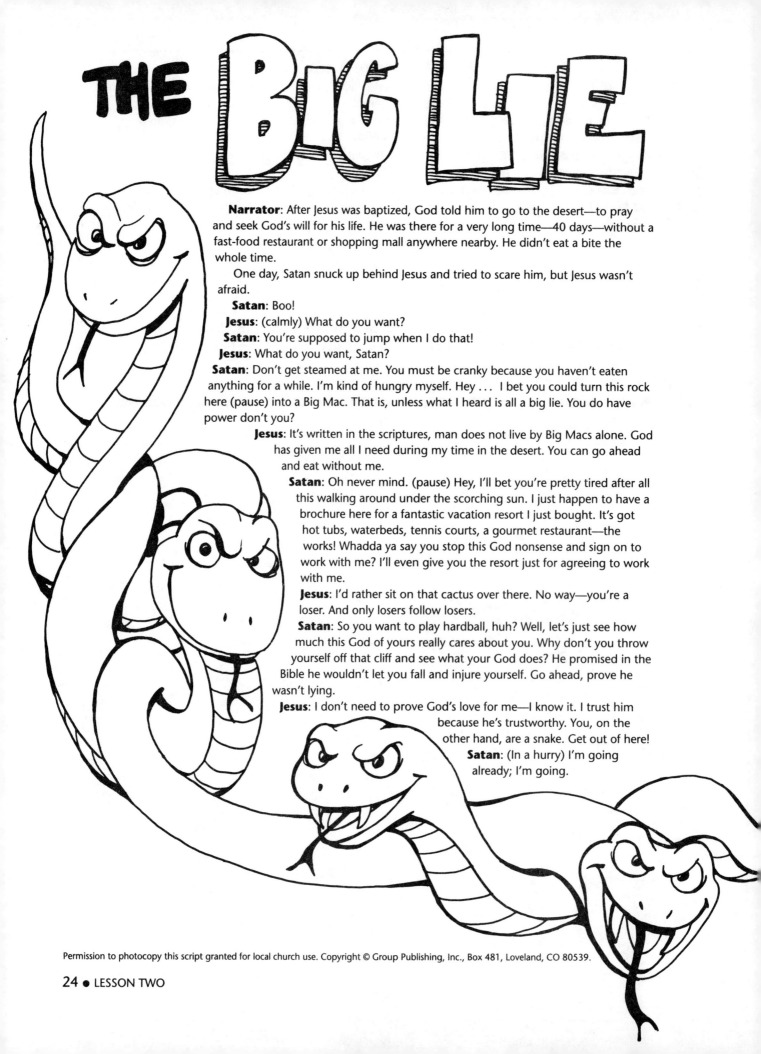

Narrator: After Jesus was baptized, God told him to go to the desert—to pray and seek God's will for his life. He was there for a very long time—40 days—without a fast-food restaurant or shopping mall anywhere nearby. He didn't eat a bite the whole time.

One day, Satan snuck up behind Jesus and tried to scare him, but Jesus wasn't afraid.

Satan: Boo!

Jesus: (calmly) What do you want?

Satan: You're supposed to jump when I do that!

Jesus: What do you want, Satan?

Satan: Don't get steamed at me. You must be cranky because you haven't eaten anything for a while. I'm kind of hungry myself. Hey . . . I bet you could turn this rock here (pause) into a Big Mac. That is, unless what I heard is all a big lie. You do have power don't you?

Jesus: It's written in the scriptures, man does not live by Big Macs alone. God has given me all I need during my time in the desert. You can go ahead and eat without me.

Satan: Oh never mind. (pause) Hey, I'll bet you're pretty tired after all this walking around under the scorching sun. I just happen to have a brochure here for a fantastic vacation resort I just bought. It's got hot tubs, waterbeds, tennis courts, a gourmet restaurant—the works! Whadda ya say you stop this God nonsense and sign on to work with me? I'll even give you the resort just for agreeing to work with me.

Jesus: I'd rather sit on that cactus over there. No way—you're a loser. And only losers follow losers.

Satan: So you want to play hardball, huh? Well, let's just see how much this God of yours really cares about you. Why don't you throw yourself off that cliff and see what your God does? He promised in the Bible he wouldn't let you fall and injure yourself. Go ahead, prove he wasn't lying.

Jesus: I don't need to prove God's love for me—I know it. I trust him because he's trustworthy. You, on the other hand, are a snake. Get out of here!

Satan: (In a hurry) I'm going already; I'm going.

LIGHT & DARK

Match each occult symbol on the right with its opposite Christian symbol on the left. Then write what each Christian symbol represents.

The pentagram is the symbol satanists stand around when they seek to contact evil spirits or want to be possessed by a demon or Satan.

The symbol of anarchy represents the rejection of all law, discipline and rules.

The "mark of the beast" or Satan is used as a general symbol of satanic involvement.

Satan is portrayed in many different ways. Often he's pictured sitting on his self-made throne.

ΙΧΘΥΣ

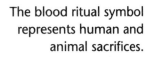

The blood ritual symbol represents human and animal sacrifices.

LESSON 3

EVIL INFLUENCES

J unior high kids are often confused, uncertain and open to a wide variety of influences. Some are good. Some are bad. The world has plenty of bad influences to offer. And sometimes it's difficult to distinguish the good from the bad. Kids need help so they can avoid the negative influences.

LESSON AIM

To help junior highers learn a Christian response to evil in the world.

OBJECTIVES

Students will:
- **learn about how evil operates in the world;**
- **see how people are taken captive by Satan's influence;**
- **discover what they know about the occult; and**
- **learn how to fight evil together.**

BIBLE BASIS
JOHN 8:42-47
COLOSSIANS 2:8-10
1 JOHN 2:15-18, 21-24

Look up the following scriptures. Then read the background paragraphs to see how the passages relate to your junior highers or middle schoolers.

In **John 8:42-47**, Jesus rebukes the Pharisees because they are like their "father, the devil"—who has no truth in him.

The Pharisees often came up with deceptive new plans to trap or trick Jesus into condemning himself or making a mistake. They were so caught up in their own hate they couldn't hear what Jesus was saying to them. His words were freeing words, but the Pharisees were deaf to them.

Just as the Pharisees tried to trick Jesus, Satan attempts to deceive Christian young people. Jesus said Satan is like a roaring lion, looking for someone to consume. Junior highers are sometimes like sheep who've lost their way, and the roaring lion is right behind them.

In **Colossians 2:8-10**, Paul warns the early Christians not to be taken in by empty deception.

Turmoil at the Colossian church prompted this letter from Paul. The church members had continued to follow worldly practices and didn't fully understand Christ's victory over the world. They were searching in the wrong places for rules for living.

Kids are searching, but the world's solutions never really fill the void inside. Some kids turn to the occult for answers. But Satan's solutions are like placebos—they look great and may give short-term comfort, but they don't treat the condition. Kids are left worse off than they were before.

In **1 John 2:15-18, 21-24**, John warns the early Christians not to love the things of the world.

The early Christians had to deal with many heresies that offered attractive temptations. John was reminding his readers that these tempting practices were false since they denied Jesus was the son of God.

But sometimes it's tough—especially for junior highers—to turn down an immediate but harmful pleasure for the sake of long-term joy. It's important that kids learn to discern truth from lies as they develop a growing relationship with Jesus.

THIS LESSON AT A GLANCE

Section	Minutes	What Students Will Do	Supplies
Opener (Option 1)	5 to 10	**Toilet Paper Slavery**—Tie each other up with toilet paper.	Blindfolds, toilet paper
(Option 2)		**Liar's Cards**—Try to figure out who's lying.	Playing cards
Action and Reflection	10 to 15	**How Much Do You Know?**—Complete a handout to determine what they know about the occult.	"Occultic Influences" handouts (p. 33), pencils
Bible Application	10 to 15	**Satan's Motives**—Discuss what Satan's motives might be.	Bibles, chalkboard or newsprint, chalk or marker, paper, pencils
Commitment	5 to 10	**Clothespin Tag**—Work as teams to try to tag each other with clothespins.	Clothespins, markers
Closing (Option 1)	5 to 10	**Building a Foundation**—Build houses with strong and weak foundations.	Playing cards, clothespins
(Option 2)		**Satan's Resume**—Write a resume for Satan.	Sample resume, paper, pencils

The Lesson

OPTION 1: TOILET PAPER SLAVERY

Form two teams. Blindfold all Team #1 members, then have them form a tight huddle and stand still with their arms down at their sides. Make sure kids on Team #1 can't see, then give kids on Team #2 each a roll of toilet paper.

Say: **Team #2, you have two minutes to tie up Team #1 with the material I've just given you. Tie them up so they can't get free. Ready? Go!**

Tell Team #2 members not to let the other team know the material is toilet paper.

After two minutes, say: **Okay. Now Team #1, you have one minute to break free from your bonds. To win, every member of your team must be free at the end of one minute. Ready? Go!**

After kids have a good laugh, have them remove their blindfolds and sit down.

Ask Team #1:

● **How did it feel to be tied up and not know what was used to tie you?** (Scary; not bad; I knew it wasn't strong stuff.)

● **If you had seen what you were tied up with, would you have fought harder to get free?** (No—I fought as hard as I could anyway; yes, I didn't realize it was just toilet paper.)

Ask Team #2:

● **Did you think the toilet paper would be strong enough to keep them tied up? Why or why not?** (Yes—it was pretty tight; no—it seemed like it would be easy to break.)

Say: **Satan's desire is to blindfold us to the truth, then tie us up in things that aren't good for us. He wants slaves who are too scared to break free of his grip. We need God's light to show us Satan's schemes and lies, or we'll never break free from them. Today, we'll look at how Satan's playground, the occult, is filled with things that look nice, but actually harm us.**

OPTION 2: LIAR'S CARDS

Form a circle and place a deck of cards face down in the center of the circle. Ask for a volunteer. Have the volunteer pick a card from the deck and look at it, not allowing anyone else to see it. Tell the volunteer you're going to ask a question about the card and that he or she may answer honestly or lie.

Ask: **Is your card higher than an eight?**

After the volunteer answers the question, have the rest of the kids vote on whether the volunteer told the truth. Then have the volunteer show his or her card.

Repeat this activity a few times.

Then ask:

● **Was it more fun to catch someone in a lie or to successfully lie yourself? Why?** (Catch someone in a lie—I like to figure out who's lying; lying—I like to fool people.)

● **How hard was it to tell who was lying and who wasn't? Explain.** (Not very hard—I could see it in their faces; very hard—there are some good liars in this group!)

Say: **Satan loves to lie. And he's good at what he does. It takes guidance and careful thought to avoid the traps he's set for us. Today we'll talk about how to recognize those traps.**

HOW MUCH DO YOU KNOW?

Form a circle and give students each an "Occultic Influences" handout (p. 33) and a pencil. Have kids each answer the questions, then refer to the answer guide and go through the questions one by one, giving the correct answers and asking students the discussion questions. Encourage kids to take notes as you discuss the answers.

ACTION AND REFLECTION
(10 to 15 minutes)

LEADER'S ANSWER GUIDE TO "OCCULTIC INFLUENCES" HANDOUT

1. d—all of the above. Kids from every social situation are involved in the occult. Some just dabble in it—playing with a Ouija board or drawing satanic symbols. Others are serious—performing blood sacrifices to Satan or constructing altars to Satan in their rooms.

Ask:

● **Why are people from every background and social situation vulnerable to the occult?** (Lots of people are looking for power or belonging; people are fascinated with dark, mysterious things.)

2. a—fascination with horoscopes. Horoscopes may seem harmless, but they teach us to trust in something other than God for our future. The more you trust the horoscopes for what's important to you, the easier it is to believe that what Satan offers will be good for you.

Ask:

● **Is there truth in horoscopes or are they just a hoax?** (There's some truth in them, sometimes my horoscope seems to fit; they're a hoax, they're wrong more often than they're right.)

Say: **Although some people claim there's validity in horoscopes, many consider them nothing more than superstition. Still others believe they're somehow tied to Satanic influences.**

3. b—*The Satanic Bible*. Written by avowed satanist Anton LaVey, *The Satanic Bible* presents "the truth according to Satan." Kids are attracted to it because it contains all kinds of evil spells and incantations— things Hollywood has glamorized in horror movies. LaVey says Satan is stronger than God, and that's why we should follow him.

Ask:

● **If you watch many horror movies, you get the idea that Satan is really stronger and more powerful than God. Is that true?** (Maybe, Satan's power can be used against God's people; no, God has proven himself stronger again and again.)

Say: **Although movies sometimes glamorize Satan's power, the Bible assures us that God's power is greater. As Jesus says in John 16:33: "In this world you will have trouble. But take heart! I have overcome the world."**

continued

4. b—False. Though not all kids who listen to heavy metal music are involved in the occult, almost all kids in the occult listen to heavy metal. Many heavy metal groups—Slayer, AC/DC, Anthrax and others—sing songs that glorify Satan, violence, murder, suicide and death. And since music is a powerful communication medium for kids, many young people adopt the values expressed in their favorite music.

Ask:

● **Do you think the music you listen to has any effect on your values? Why or why not?** (No, music is just something to listen to; yes, if you listen to it enough, it'll affect the way you look at things.)

5. a—True. The world seems out of control and dangerous to young teenagers. One way to battle fear is to gain power. And kids need to feel a sense of belonging. Satan offers magical, dark powers and a feeling of importance. But the powers are destructive, and the feeling of importance is false.

Ask:

● **When you feel powerless or afraid, who or what do you turn to?** (My parents; friends; books; God.)

6. c and d—The Ouija board and fantasy role-playing games. The Ouija board is a popular game with kids. You ask the board a question and an evil spirit is supposed to give you the answer. Fantasy role-playing games are controversial games that many kids in the occult play. The games require each player to take on and act out a role in an imaginary adventure. For some kids, the games are harmless. For others, the games lure them into trusting Satan for guidance and power.

Ask:

● **Why is it dangerous to look for answers from "mysterious forces" and not God?** (You could be trusting in something that's not real; you might believe something is true about yourself that isn't true.)

7. b—False. Church involvement is no guarantee that kids won't get involved in the occult. Often kids who are interested in the occult will go to church because they're fascinated with religious symbolism. The occult—which means "secret" or "hidden"—is a religion, and it creates much of its content by twisting Christian practices.

Ask:

● **Can church involvement help you avoid the occult? Explain.** (Yes, learning more about God can help you grow in your faith so you can stand up to occult temptations; no, if you don't believe in God, being involved in church won't help.)

8. b—False. Some of the so-called "black metal" bands claim they don't actually practice what they preach. Even Slayer, widely recognized as the most overtly satanist band, says its occultic songs and performances are simply an act designed to draw crowds. Money is their motive. But the kids who listen to black metal bands believe what they hear, and many are drawn into the occult.

Ask:

● **Is it wrong for groups like Slayer to sing about Satan if the band members don't really practice the occult? Why or why not?** (Yes, they have a bad effect on the people who listen to them; no, music is just entertainment.)

9. b—False. Even though the occult is like an addictive drug, kids can be set free from its influence. But like people who withdraw from addiction to alcohol or drugs, kids who pull out of the occult must stay away from all occultic influences. These include most horror movies, movies with occultic themes, black metal music and satanist literature.

Ask:

● **What's the first step someone who's involved in the occult should take to get out?** (Confess belief in Jesus; get with other Christians who can help; ask God for forgiveness.)

SATAN'S MOTIVES

Form groups of three. Have each group read aloud the following scriptures:

- John 8:42-47
- 1 John 2:15-18, 21-24
- Colossians 2:8-10

While groups are reading, write the following discussion questions on a chalkboard or newsprint:

- If Satan is so deceptive, why doesn't God let us know we're being deceived by him?
- Does Satan believe in God? Why or why not?
- What's Satan's primary mission on Earth?
- What are three ways people today are "taken captive through hollow and deceptive philosophy"?

Give groups each a piece of paper and a pencil. Ask them to discuss the questions and write their answers. Then gather kids together and have a spokesperson from each group explain the group's answers.

CLOTHESPIN TAG

Form the same groups of three you had in the last activity. Give each person a clothespin and each group a different-color marker. Have kids each mark their clothespin with their group's marker.

Say: **The goal of this game is to clip your clothespin onto somebody's clothing while not allowing anyone to clip a clothespin onto you. You may not remove a clothespin once it's clipped to you. When I shout "Stop," the team with the fewest clothespins stuck to its team members wins. Your team has one minute to develop a strategy for the game.**

Wait one minute, then shout, **"Go!"**

After a couple of minutes, shout, **"Stop!"**

Say: **The best way to win this game is to circle together—so you can guard one another from behind. And the best way to fight occultic influences is to help each other. You can't always see that something's bad for you—so let other Christian friends, your parents and caring adults help you fight temptation.**

Write on your clothespin one way you can resist the influence of the occult in your life. Then take it home as a reminder.

Have kids talk in their threesomes about how they can be a protection for each other against the occult. Then have them each thank the other members of their threesome for supporting them in the fight against evil.

OPTION 1: BUILDING A FOUNDATION

Read aloud Luke 6:46-49. Form two teams. Have one team build a house out of playing cards or other game cards. Have the other team build a house out of clothespins. Then have the opposing teams each blow on the other's houses to see which will stand.

Say: **The only foundation in our life that will stand is a commitment to follow Jesus. When life gets hard and temptations are strong, your relationship with God can pull you through.**

Close by asking kids to each thank God for one way he's made their foundation strong.

OPTION 2: SATAN'S RESUME

Form three groups and give each group a copy of a sample resume. Have each group write one of the following parts of Satan's resume, using the sample as a guide:

- Group #1—Satan's education;
- Group #2—Satan's work experience; and
- Group #3—Satan's interests and hobbies.

After three minutes, have groups each share their portion of the resume.

Say: **Satan's resume qualifies him as leader of the occult but little else. When we consider who to have at the center of our lives, we should look instead at God's resume.**

Close by reading aloud God's resume from Psalm 145:8-21.

If You Still Have Time . . .

Sunday's On the Way—Perform a pantomime to Carman's song "Sunday's On the Way," from the album of the same name. Listen to the song once, then ask for four volunteers to play Satan, Jesus, Grave and Gabriel. Use black plastic trash bags for Satan's and Grave's costumes. Use white sheets for Jesus' and Gabriel's costumes. Play the song again and have volunteers pantomime the words.

Balloon Bouquets—Bring one package of multicolor balloons and one package of dark-color balloons. Have the kids write God's characteristics on the multicolor balloons and Satan's characteristics on the dark-color balloons. Hang the multicolor balloons in your meeting room. Have the kids pop the dark-color ones.

OCCULTIC INFLUENCES

Circle the correct answer or answers.

1. Many kids who get involved in the occult come from:
   - a. low-income families
   - b. middle-class families
   - c. upper-class families
   - d. all of the above

2. An early sign of involvement in the occult might be:
   - a. fascination with horoscopes
   - b. wearing a black T-shirt
   - c. sleeplessness
   - d. repeated vomiting
   - e. all of the above
   - f. none of the above

3. The most popular book among people who dabble in the occult is:
   - a. *Flowers In the Attic*
   - b. *The Satanic Bible*
   - c. *Bible*
   - d. all of the above
   - e. none of the above

4. There's no connection between heavy metal music and occultism.
   - a. True
   - b. False

5. The main reason junior highers get involved with the occult is because they're looking for a source of power or a sense of belonging.
   - a. True
   - b. False

6. Games that have been tied to occult involvement include:
   - a. Monopoly
   - b. Uno
   - c. Ouija board
   - d. fantasy role-playing games
   - e. Trivial Pursuit
   - f. video games
   - g. all of the above
   - h. none of the above

7. It's impossible for someone who goes to church to get involved in the occult.
   - a. True
   - b. False

8. All the heavy metal bands that sing about Satan and evil are actively involved in the occult.
   - a. True
   - b. False

9. Once a person is hooked on the occult, it's impossible for him or her to get out of it.
   - a. True
   - b. False

LESSON 4

STRENGTH TO OVERCOME THE FEAR

The dark power and mystery of the occult and evil can scare junior highers. They need to be reminded that God has promised comfort, assurance and strength to those who follow him.

Kids don't have to live in fear of Satan because Jesus has already fought and defeated him.

LESSON AIM

To show junior highers how to draw strength from God and overcome their fears of the occult and the unknown.

OBJECTIVES

Students will:
● learn how to depend upon God to counter their fears;
● see how Jesus can help in their troubles;
● understand that nothing can separate them from God's love; and
● learn how God's Word can give them comfort in the midst of fear.

BIBLE BASIS
PSALM 23
JOHN 16:33
ROMANS 8:31-39

Look up the following scriptures. Then read the background paragraphs to see how the passages relate to your junior highers or middle schoolers.

Psalm 23 states: "Though I walk through the valley of the shadow of death, I will fear no evil."

The Psalmist uses familiar imagery—shepherds and sheep—to convey God's care over his children. The Psalmist promises peace in the midst of a world filled with anxiety.

Kids sometimes feel anxious about what's ahead. They

think they have to find their own way in a dangerous world. But they're not alone. If they'll seek God and depend upon him for guidance, they can confront the world's dangers and conquer their temptations.

In **John 16:33**, John says Christians will have trouble, but Jesus has already overcome the world.

Jesus is realistic. Life isn't going to be easy. There are fears and evil influences everywhere. But he's already faced those foes and won.

When kids feel overwhelmed by the presence of evil in the world, they can take comfort that Jesus offers strength to face life's troubles.

In **Romans 8:31-39**, Paul says if God is for us, who can be against us?

The early Christians in Rome were so harshly persecuted they fled underground to the catacombs to meet. They feared for their lives every day. Often, it must have seemed God had forgotten about them. But he hadn't.

It's easy to lose perspective in the midst of fear and trouble. Young people need assurance that God will protect and sustain them against evil's influence.

THIS LESSON AT A GLANCE

Section	Minutes	What Students Will Do	Supplies
Opener (Option 1)	5 to 10	**Light Relay**—Run a relay race with candles.	Candles, cardboard, matches
(Option 2)		**Bursting Satan's Bubble**—Design and pop a model of Satan's world.	Balloons, magazines, tape, pins
Action and Reflection	10 to 15	**The Dark Valley Maze**—Find a solution to a maze.	"Dark Valley Maze" handouts (p. 41), pencils
Bible Application	10 to 15	**Fear No Evil**—Write reasons they can feel assured of God's protection.	Bibles, paper, pencils
Commitment	5 to 10	**Conquering Fears**—Evaluate their fears and find one comforting truth in the Bible.	Bibles, paper, pencils, chalkboard or newsprint, chalk or marker
Closing (Option 1)	5 to 10	**Paper Plate Praise**—Toss paper plates to symbolize freedom from evil influences.	Paper plates, markers, rocks, tape
(Option 2)		**Candle Thanks**—Give thanks to God by singing and lighting candles.	Candles, cardboard, matches

The Lesson

O P E N E R
(5 to 10 minutes)

OPTION 1: LIGHT RELAY

You might want to move to an uncarpeted, large room for this activity. Close any curtains and block out as much light as possible. Form two equal-size teams, and give each student a candle and a wax catcher—a small circle of cardboard around the candle. Have both teams line up single file on one side of the room. Light one large candle and place it on a table—or hold it yourself—at the opposite side of the room from the kids.

Say: **This is a light relay. The first person in each line will race to the lit candle, light his or her candle, then carefully *walk* back to his or her team and light the candle of the next person in line. Then the two of you will lock arms and walk—with your lit candles—to the big candle at the end of the room and back. Each time you return to your team, light the next person's candle, lock arms, and walk to the big candle and back.**

If your candle goes out at any point, the whole team must stop, relight your candle, then continue. Don't let your candle get too close to any clothing, and don't run because you'll blow out your flame. The first team to have all its members lock arms with lit candles and go to the big candle and back wins.

Turn out the lights, then begin the race.

Afterward, ask:

● **How did the brightness of the room change as the game progressed?**

● **How did you feel as the room got brighter?** (Confident; I could see better.)

Say: **Evil has made the world a dark place. But a light has come into the world, and that light is stronger than the darkness. That light is Jesus. As we come to him for strength and pass that strength on to others—just like our light relay—we're able to push back the darkness.**

OPTION 2: BURSTING SATAN'S BUBBLE

Form groups of three. Give each group a balloon, three magazines and tape. Ask groups to choose pictures or articles that depict evil in the world. Then have them each blow up their balloon and tape the pictures and articles to it to form "Satan's World."

Then read aloud Hebrews 4:12-13.

Say: **Though Satan would like you to think he controls the world, he doesn't. Jesus died and rose again to take away Satan's power over you and me. And God's Word—**

the Bible—can give us confidence to battle Satan and his works in the world. For God's Word is sharper than a two-edged sword.

Give students each a pin. Have them pop their group's balloon at the count of three to symbolize God's sword—the Bible—piercing Satan's lies.

THE DARK VALLEY MAZE

Give each person a copy of the "Dark Valley Maze" (p. 41) and a pencil. Have kids each complete the maze. Ask the first person who finishes the maze to go to all the other students and show them the correct path through it. That person should keep showing people the solution until everyone has finished.

Ask:

● **How did it feel to know someone made it through the maze before you? Why?** (Good, then I knew it could be done; bad, I wanted to be first.)

● **If you finished first, how did you feel about helping others find their way through the maze?** (Good, I could help out people who were stuck; bad, I didn't want them to feel embarrassed.)

● **If you didn't finish first, how did you feel when you received help?** (Good—I really needed the help; bad—I wanted to finish it myself.)

● **How are the dead ends in this maze like the confrontations you have with temptation or evil?** (They're like traps; you have to plan ahead to avoid them.)

● **How do you feel when you can't find a way out of a difficult situation?** (Uncomfortable; frustrated; angry.)

Say: **Just as someone made it through the maze first and came back to help you, so Jesus has confronted evil and overcome it. Now he's here to help you find your way through the maze of temptations and evil around you. There's always a way out of the maze if you have Jesus to help you.**

FEAR NO EVIL

Form a circle and give each person a Bible, a piece of paper and a pencil. Have volunteers read aloud Psalm 23 and John 16:33.

Ask:

● **How do you know Jesus has "overcome the world"— we still have trouble in the world, don't we?** (Jesus died for our sins, but there's still sin in the world; because the Bible tells us.)

● **What is "the valley of the shadow of death"?** (Evil; problems people face.)

● **What are dangers you face in your "valley"?** (Getting in with the wrong crowd; temptation to do wrong.)

ACTION AND REFLECTION
(10 to 15 minutes)

BIBLE APPLICATION
(10 to 15 minutes)

● **Why can we feel safe when we're walking through "the valley of the shadow of death"?** (Because Jesus will be there with us, guiding us.)

Say: **On your paper, write one thing that might endanger your relationship with God.**

Have a volunteer read aloud Romans 8:31-39.

Ask:

● **What does "If God is for us, who can be against us" mean?** (God is stronger than any trouble or enemy.)

Say: **Reread Romans 8:38-39. Nothing—not even Satan—can keep God's love from you. Only you can separate yourself from him. He wants to be near you to protect and guide you always.**

Form a circle. Join kids as they lock arms. Say: **God's love is powerful. And as we look to him for strength, we can also count on each other for support.**

Have kids keep their feet still and lean back with their arms locked. Remind them this is a time to be serious—not to goof off. After a few seconds, have everyone stand up straight and unlock their arms. Say: **Support for one another allowed us to lean back without falling. In the same way, supporting each other can help us not fear evil but trust in God.**

Have kids each tell the person on their right "thanks" for supporting them in this circle and in the future as they face fears and temptations.

COMMITMENT
(5 to 10 minutes)

CONQUERING FEARS

Give students each a Bible, a piece of paper and a pencil. Have students each bow their head and close their eyes.

Say: **I'm going to read a list of fears. If I read something that scares you, raise your hand. Make sure you keep your eyes closed and your head bowed as we do this.**

Read aloud the following fears:

● **I'm afraid my parents might die somehow.**

● **I'm afraid I won't get the grades I want in school.**

● **I'm afraid I'll have to fight in a war someday.**

● **I'm afraid I'll give in to some temptation in my life right now.**

● **I'm afraid of the violence in the world.**

● **I'm afraid sometimes that Satan really is more powerful than God.**

● **I'm afraid my sins are so bad that God has a hard time loving me.**

● **I'm afraid of being lonely.**

● **I'm afraid my friends will reject me if I follow God's ways more closely.**

● **I'm afraid I'll never find what I really want to do in life.**

Ask kids each to write on their paper the one thing they fear the most—whether it's something you've named or not.

Write on a chalkboard or newsprint the scripture references you read in the previous activity: Psalm 23; John 16:33; and Romans 8:31-39.

Say: **Look at the scriptures we read a few minutes ago. Write one truth from these scriptures that can help you face the thing you fear most in life. Then spend a couple of minutes in silent prayer—asking God to conquer your fears with his truth.**

Table Talk

The Table Talk activity in this course helps junior highers and middle schoolers talk about evil and the occult with their parents.

If you choose to use the Table Talk activity, this is a good time to show students the "Table Talk" handout (p. 42). Ask them to spend time with their parents completing it.

Before kids leave, give them each the "Table Talk" handout to take home or tell them you'll be sending it to their parents.

Or use the Table Talk idea found in the Bonus Ideas (p. 43) for a meeting based on the handout.

OPTION 1: PAPER PLATE PRAISE

Give students each a heavy-duty paper plate, a marker and a rock. Have them each list on their plate three reasons God can be trusted to take care of them. Then have kids each tape their rock to the bottom of their plate. Take them outside and have them try to fly their plates like a Frisbee.

After a few unsuccessful flights, ask:

● **How is the rock taped to your plate like evil's influence in your life?** (It weighs me down and keeps me from flying.)

Say: **When the evil in the world brings you down—like these rocks—get away from its influence and draw close to God through prayer, Bible reading and time with other Christians.**

Have students remove the rocks and fly their plates. Then close with a prayer of thanksgiving for God's protection and love.

OPTION 2: CANDLE THANKS

Form a circle, and give each student an unlit candle with a wax catcher. Light a large candle and place it in the middle of the circle. Together, sing "Alleluia" or another familiar chorus. During the song, have each young person—one at a time—light his or her candle from the candle in the middle. When everyone has a lit candle, close with a prayer of thanksgiving for God's protection and love.

CLOSING
(5 to 10 minutes)

If You Still Have Time . . .

Paper Bouquets—Thank God for overcoming the power of the occult by presenting him with a paper bouquet of balloons. Give kids each a paper plate and a marker. Have them each draw a balloon on their plate, then write "God, I love you because . . ." and finish the sentence. Attach all the plates together with a stapler or glue, add a string to each and tape the bouquet to a meeting room wall.

Course Reflection—Form a circle. Ask students to reflect on the past four lessons. Have them take turns completing the following sentences:

- Something I learned in this course was . . .
- If I could tell my friends about this course, I'd say . . .
- Something I'll do differently because of this course is . . .

DARK VALLEY MAZE

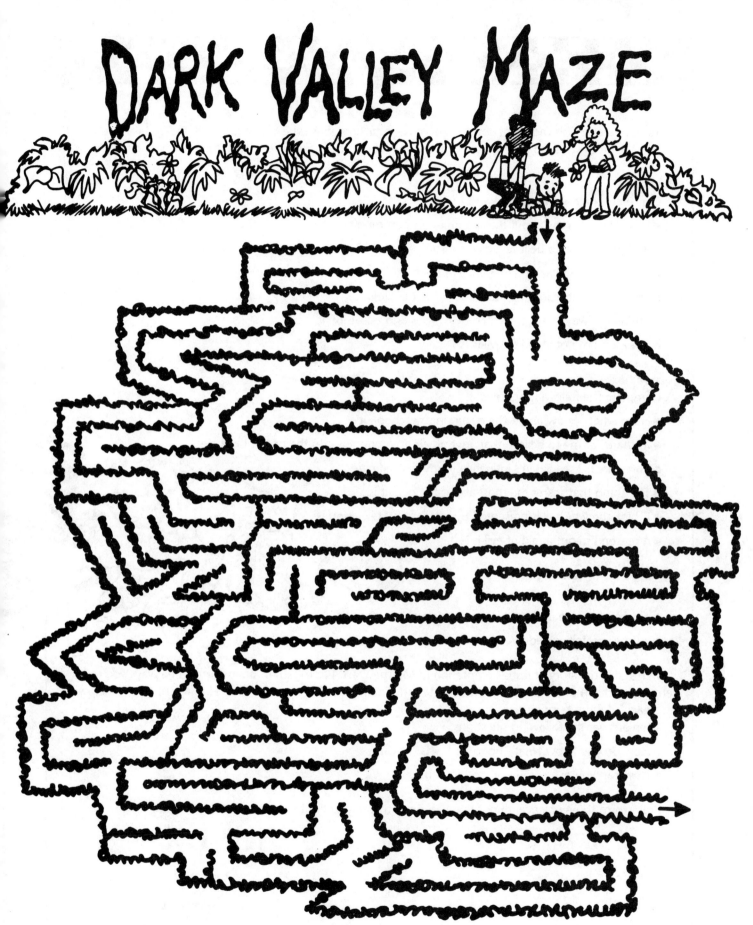

Table Talk

To the Parent: This month at church, we've been talking about the occult and evil. Please take a few minutes to sit down with your junior higher to talk about these topics. Use this sheet to spark discussion.

Parent

Complete the following sentences:

● From what I know about the occult in our community, it's . . .

● It's hard for me to believe kids are into the occult because . . .

● Three areas I see Satan's influence in the world are . . .

● The thing that scares me most about the occult is . . .

● I think the way evil is presented by movies and television is . . .

● A reason I'm not afraid of evil is . . .

Junior higher

Complete the following sentences:

● From what I know about the occult in my school, it's . . .

● It's hard for me to believe that anybody in my school is into the occult because . . .

● Three areas I see Satan's influence in my daily life are . . .

● The thing that scares me most about the occult is . . .

● I think the way evil is presented by movies and television is . . .

● A reason I'm not afraid of evil is . . .

Parent and junior higher

Tell about:

● a time you were intrigued by something evil or occultic.

● a time you felt scared by something evil.

Talk about the story of Jesus' temptation in Matthew 4:1-11. Together, brainstorm three ways you're tempted today that are similar to the temptations Satan placed in front of Jesus. Find a scripture to help you face each of these temptations.

Then answer the following questions:

● How do you know what's good and what's evil?

● How can you overcome evil around you?

Brainstorm three practical things you can do as a family to fight the evil influences in your world.

BONUS IDEAS

Satan's Library—Take your kids to a bookstore or library. Have them scatter and list as many occult-related books as they can find. Then, as a group, compose a letter of thanks if the store has few occultic resources or a letter of complaint if the store has many occultic resources.

Fantasy Role-Playing Meeting—Have kids compare other popular games to the fantasy role-playing games. Plan a game night. Borrow a fantasy role-playing game such as Dungeons & Dragons and three or four other popular games such as Monopoly, Pictionary, Balderdash or Clue. Have kids rotate in groups, playing each game. Then have a group discussion about the games.

Ask:
- **How did the fantasy role-playing game differ from the other games?**
- **Which games teach negative values? Explain.**
- **Which games teach positive values? Explain.**
- **Could fantasy role-playing games be used to get young people interested in the occult? Why or why not?**

Turning the Occult Inside Out—Copy the lyrics from a black metal song by groups such as Blood Feast, Slayer or Megadeth. Then have kids write lyrics that communicate the exact opposite—or Christian—message.

Table Talk—Use the "Table Talk" handout (p. 42) for a parents and kids' meeting. Invite church staff members to attend. Have parents and kids each complete the handout and discuss it. As a group, decide how you'll take action to minimize occultic influences in your community or in the media. Close the meeting with a time of worship and thankfulness to God for overcoming evil.

The Occult Risk Profile—Give kids "The Occult Risk Profile" questionnaire (p. 46) to see how well they can identify a person with a high risk of involvement in the occult.

Saying No to Satan—Using the story of Jesus' temptation in the wilderness (Matthew 4:1-11), have kids form groups and brainstorm the design for a "Just Say No to Satan" poster. Give groups markers, posterboard, magazines, construction paper and glue. Then have groups each display and talk about their poster. Hang the posters in your meeting room, in kids' schools or in public places (if you have permission).

BONUS IDEAS ● 43

Parental Prevention—Meet with parents to talk about warning signs of occult involvement. Signs include:
- immersion in heavy metal and black metal music;
- occult-oriented possessions, particularly jewelry with occultic symbols;
- interest in books on subjects such as demon possession, rituals, chants and spells;
- involvement with occultic games, including tarot cards, Ouija boards and sometimes Dungeons & Dragons;
- drug or alcohol abuse;
- severe personality changes, including declining grades, violent rages, withdrawal from friends and family; and
- physical mutilation, including scars where blood sacrifices are taken, occultic tattoos and missing finger tips where a flesh sacrifice was taken.

Then have parents express their feelings about the occult by finishing the following statements:
- The thing that frightens me about the occult is . . .
- I think young people turn to the occult because . . .
- The occult makes me angry because . . .

The Lion, the Witch and the Wardrobe—Rent or purchase the video version of C.S. Lewis' *The Lion, the Witch and the Wardrobe*. Watch it with your students, then discuss Christ's victory over Satan.

Make-Our-Own-Symbol—Give kids each construction paper, posterboard, a marker and scissors. Have kids each design and display their own Christian symbol, using the "Light and Dark" handout (p. 25) for ideas.

Occultic Scavenger Hunt—Take kids to a mall or shopping center. Form pairs, then give each pair the following list of items to find. When kids find an item, they should write the store name they found it in and the price. Tell everyone to meet at a specified location and time, then set them loose to find the occultic items. The pair that finds the most items on the list wins.
- a Slayer T-Shirt
- a Megadeth record album
- an occultic fiction novel
- an ad for a horror movie
- a copy of *The Satanic Bible*
- 666 on a piece of jewelry
- a goat's head in any form

Discuss the influence of the occult in the media, fashion and literature. Talk about how kids can influence stores and manufacturers not to produce occult-related items.

Neewollah Party—Neewollah is Halloween spelled backward. So have a backward Halloween party with the following activities:

- Instead of carving jack-o-lanterns, have kids carve into pumpkins words representing the fruit of the Spirit.
- Instead of scary music, have kids listen to Christian music or a humorous album by Ken Davis.
- Instead of trick-or-treat, have kids create uplifting posters and then give them to one another.
- Instead of dressing up as ghouls, have kids dress up as Bible characters.

Satan in the World Retreat—Bring examples of magazines, newspapers, books, music, videos and TV soap operas (if you secure appropriate copyright permission). Set aside time to focus on each medium, and have kids look for occultic influences in each one.

For example, form groups and give each group a stack of newspapers. Have kids make a posterboard collage of all the articles they find that illustrate Satan's influence in the world.

Have kids watch a short segment of a popular soap opera. Then have groups act out the scene you watched—with a twist: Have them do it the way Christian characters would behave and react.

Read a short segment of a book that's tainted by occultic influences, such as one of Stephen King's popular books. Then contrast it by reading a segment of a Christian novel, such as one of George MacDonald's books.

Watch *Chariots of Fire*, then compare it with a popular horror movie. Have kids decide what the focus and message of each movie is. Then have them read aloud Philippians 4:8. See how well each movie fits into Paul's guidelines for living.

Close the retreat with a celebration featuring uplifting games and Christian music.

PARTY PLEASER

RETREAT IDEA

THE OCCULT RISK PROFILE

DANGER

POISON

WATCH OUT!

WARNING

STOP

GO BACK

Mark the answers that best describe a person with a high risk of getting involved in the occult.

1. Favorite kind of movie:
❏ comedy ❏ action/adventure ❏ horror ❏ suspense ❏ drama

2. Favorite kind of music:
❏ new wave ❏ classic rock ❏ top 40 ❏ heavy metal
❏ black metal ❏ country ❏ rhythm and blues ❏ Latin

3. Favorite kind of book:
❏ mystery ❏ adventure ❏ biography ❏ sports
❏ horror ❏ suspense ❏ romance ❏ history

4. Has experimented with:
❏ alcohol ❏ marijuana ❏ crack or cocaine ❏ sniffing glue
❏ hard drugs such as heroin or LSD

5. Is interested in death and dead things:
❏ usually ❏ sometimes ❏ never

6. Is mostly:
❏ withdrawn ❏ outgoing

7. Favorite free-time activity:
❏ sports ❏ watching television ❏ reading novels
❏ playing fantasy role-playing games

How would you answer these questions? How would your friends answer them? Use this guide to check the occult risk factor:

Six to seven high-risk answers—high probability of current occult involvement.
Three to five high-risk answers—moderate risk and possibly getting more involved in occult practices.
Zero to two high-risk answers—little or no risk of involvement. Many people have some fascination with horror or fantasy but no inclination to get involved with the occult.

High-Risk Answers:

1. horror; 2. black metal, sometimes heavy metal; 3. horror; 4. any drug, but especially hard drugs; 5. usually or sometimes; 6. withdrawn; 7. playing fantasy role-playing games.

More from Group's Active Bible Curriculum

Yes, I want Scripture-based learning that blasts away boredom.

For Senior High

Quantity

_____	207-2	**Counterfeit Religions** ISBN 1-55945-207-2 $6.95
_____	202-1	**Getting Along With Parents** ISBN 1-55945-202-1 $6.95
_____	208-0	**The Gospel of John: Jesus' Teachings** ISBN 1-55945-208-0 $6.95
_____	200-5	**Hazardous to Your Health** ISBN 1-55945-200-5 $6.95
_____	203-X	**Is Marriage in Your Future?** ISBN 1-55945-203-X $6.95
_____	205-6	**Knowing God's Will** ISBN 1-55945-205-6 $6.95
_____	201-3	**School Struggles** ISBN 1-55945-201-3 $6.95
_____	206-4	**Sex: A Christian Perspective** ISBN 1-55945-206-4 $6.95
_____	204-8	**Your Life as a Disciple** ISBN 1-55945-204-8 $6.95

For Junior High/Middle School

Quantity

_____	100-9	**Boosting Self-Esteem** ISBN 1-55945-100-9 $6.95
_____	118-1	**Drugs & Drinking** ISBN 1-55945-118-1 $6.95
_____	102-5	**Evil and the Occult** ISBN 1-55945-102-5 $6.95
_____	108-4	**Is God Unfair?** ISBN 1-55945-108-4 $6.95
_____	107-6	**Making Parents Proud** ISBN 1-55945-107-6 $6.95
_____	103-3	**Peer Pressure** ISBN 1-55945-103-3 $6.95
_____	104-1	**Prayer** ISBN 1-55945-104-1 $6.95
_____	101-7	**Today's Music: Good or Bad?** ISBN 1-55945-101-7 $6.95
_____	105-X	**What's a Christian?** ISBN 1-55945-105-X $6.95

Yes, please send me _____ of Group's Active Bible Curriculum™ studies at $6.95 each plus $3 postage and handling per order. Colorado residents add 3% sales tax.

03151

▸ ☐ Check enclosed ☐ VISA ☐ MasterCard

Credit card # _____

Expires _____

(Please print)

Name _____

Address _____

City _____

State _____ ZIP _____

Daytime phone (___) _____

Take this order form or a photocopy to your favorite Christian bookstore. Or mail to:

Group's Active Bible Curriculum
Box 481 ● Loveland, CO 80539 ● (303) 669-3836

Blast away boredom with these upcoming scripture-based topics.

For Senior High:

- Dating
- Making decisions
- Materialism

- New Age
- Being a servant
- Injustice

- Who is God?
- Music and media
- Faith in tough times

For Junior High:

- Success in school
- Independence
- Body-health

- Miracles
- Relationships: Guys and girls
- Sharing faith

- Handling conflict
- Creation
- The Bible

For more details write:

Box 481 ● Loveland, CO 80539 ● 800-747-6060